Library of Congress Cataloging-in-Publication Data

Back, Christine.
    Chicken and egg.

    (Stopwatch books)
    Includes index.
    Summary: Photographs, drawings, and text on two
different levels of difficulty follow the development
of a chick embryo from the fertilization and laying
of an egg to the time the chick hatches.
        I. Chickens—Development—Juvenile literature.
2. Eggs—Juvenile literature. [I. Chick embryo.
2. Reproduction. 3. Eggs] I. Olesen, Jens.
II. Jarner, Bo, ill. III. Title. IV. Series.
SF487.5.B33 1986   598'.617   86-10019
ISBN 0-382-09292-9
ISBN 0-382-09284-8 (lib. bdg.)

English edition first published by A & C Black (Publishers) Limited
35 Bedford Row, London WC1R 4JH

English edition © 1984 A & C Black (Publishers) Limited
First published 1982 by Forlaget Apostrof, Copenhagen, Denmark, under the title
'Der er en kylling i aegget'.
© 1982 Forlaget Apostrof

First published in the United States in 1986
by Silver Burdett Company
Morristown, New Jersey

Acknowledgements
The artwork is by B L Kearley Ltd.
Photograph on page 4, Farmer's Weekly.
Photograph on page 6, G I Bernard/Oxford Scientific Films.

Stopwatch books

Chicken and egg

Christine Back and Jens Olesen
Photographs by Bo Jarner

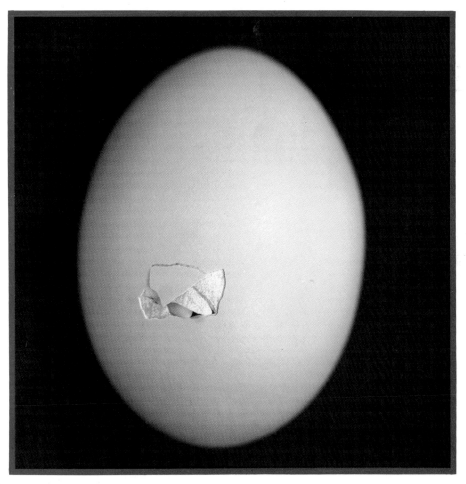

 Silver Burdett Company • Morristown, New Jersey

Here is a hen's egg.

A hen lays eggs nearly every day. Most of the eggs are packed in boxes and taken to food stores. Then we buy the eggs and eat them.

Do you ever have eggs for breakfast?

Some hen's eggs are not for eating and we cannot buy them in the store. These eggs will hatch into chicks.

This book tells you how a chick comes from one of these eggs.

Here are a hen and a rooster.

Look at the drawing.

Hen

Rooster

The hen is a female bird. The rooster is a male bird.
Can you see the rooster's long tail feathers?

Now look at the photograph. This hen and rooster are
going to mate. When the birds have mated, the hen will
lay special eggs. These eggs will hatch into chicks.
The hen will be the mother of the chicks and the
rooster will be the father.

The hen makes a nest for her eggs.

Each day, the hen lays one egg in her nest.
After ten days, there are ten eggs in the nest.

Here are the hen's eggs.

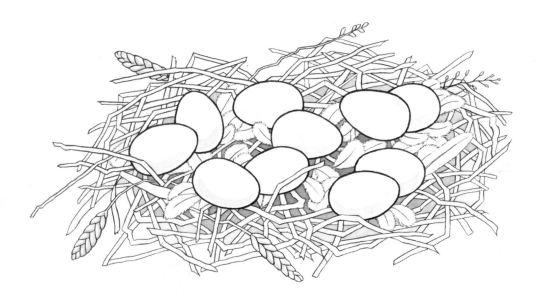

Now the hen sits on her eggs to keep them warm.
Inside each egg, a chick will soon begin to grow.
If the eggs get cold the chicks will die.
The hen leaves her nest to find food, but she soon
goes back to sit on her eggs.

This egg has just been laid.

Look at the photograph. Around the outside of the egg there is a hard shell. Part of this shell has been taken away so that you can see inside the egg.

The yellow part of the egg is called the yolk.
The part around the yolk is called the white.

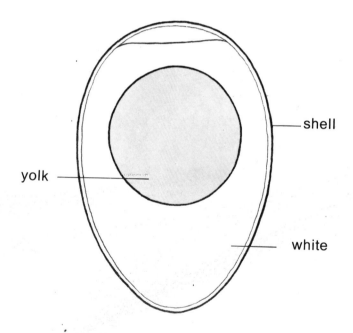

This egg is not for eating. On the yolk of the egg, a tiny spot will soon begin to grow. The spot will grow into a chick.

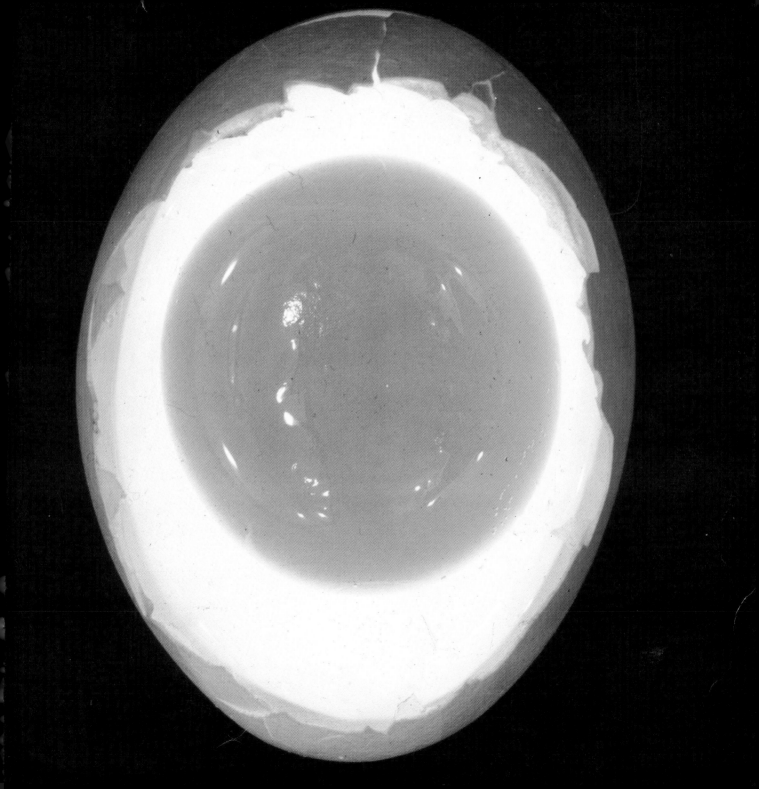

A chick is growing inside the egg.

For three days the hen has been keeping the eggs warm.
She keeps turning the eggs around so that they
will be warm all over.

Look at the photograph. You can see inside one of the
hen's eggs. Can you see the red lines on the yolk?
This tells you that a chick is beginning to grow there.

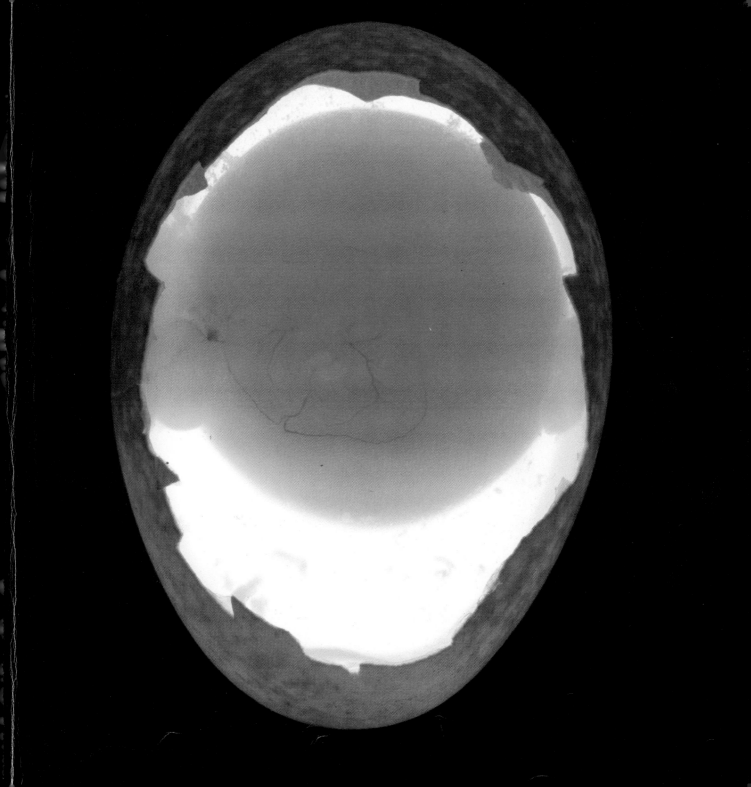

The chick has been growing for six days.

Here is the chick on the yolk of the egg.

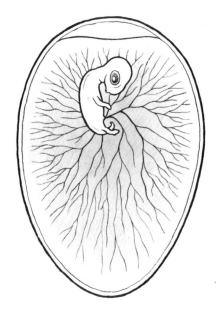

Can you see the chick's head and eye?

Now look at the photograph. The black spot near the top of the yolk is the chick's eye.

The chick needs food and air to live and grow.
The chick's food comes from the yolk of the egg.
Air comes into the egg through tiny holes in the shell.
Can you see the red lines on the yolk of the egg?
These are tubes that carry food and air to the chick.

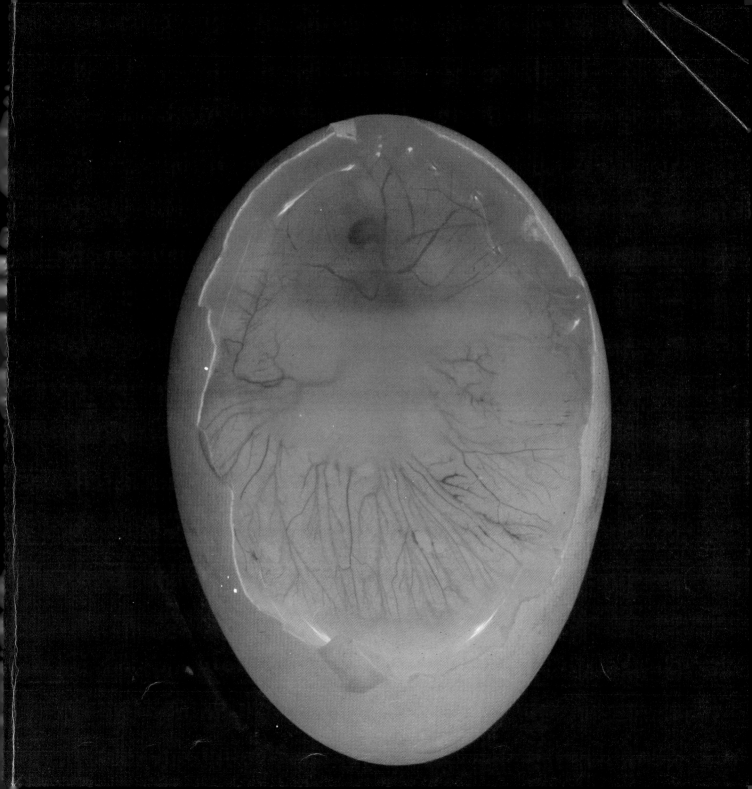

The chick grows bigger.

The hen has been sitting on the egg for nine days.

Here is the chick inside the egg.

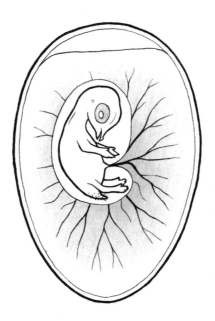

Now the chick looks like a little bird. Can you see
its beak? The chick floats in a bag of water called
a sac. If the egg is bumped the chick will not be hurt.

Look at the photograph. Can you see the tubes that carry
food and air to the chick? They have grown bigger.
You cannot see the chick yet, it is hidden inside the egg.

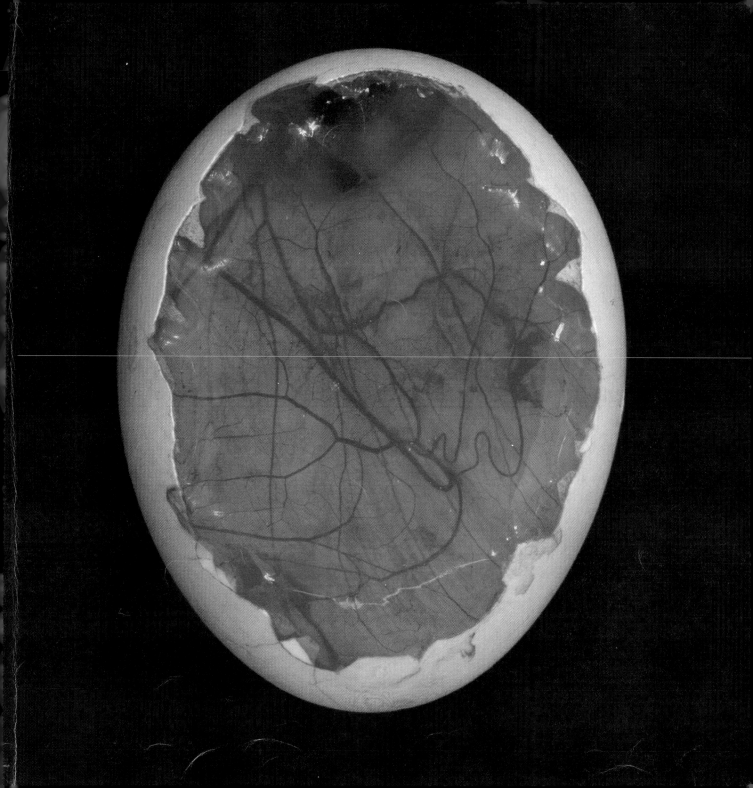

The chick is nearly ready to come out of the egg.

The chick has been growing for eighteen days.

Can you see the sac that protects the chick?

Now look at the big photograph. The sac has been taken away so that you can see the chick properly. Can you see the chick's feathers and its big feet? Near the end of the chick's beak there is a bump called the egg tooth.

The chick breaks the eggshell.

After twenty-one days, the chick is ready to hatch out of the egg. The chick uses its egg tooth to tap the shell. Soon it makes a tiny hole in the shell.

The chick keeps tapping and the hole gets bigger . . .

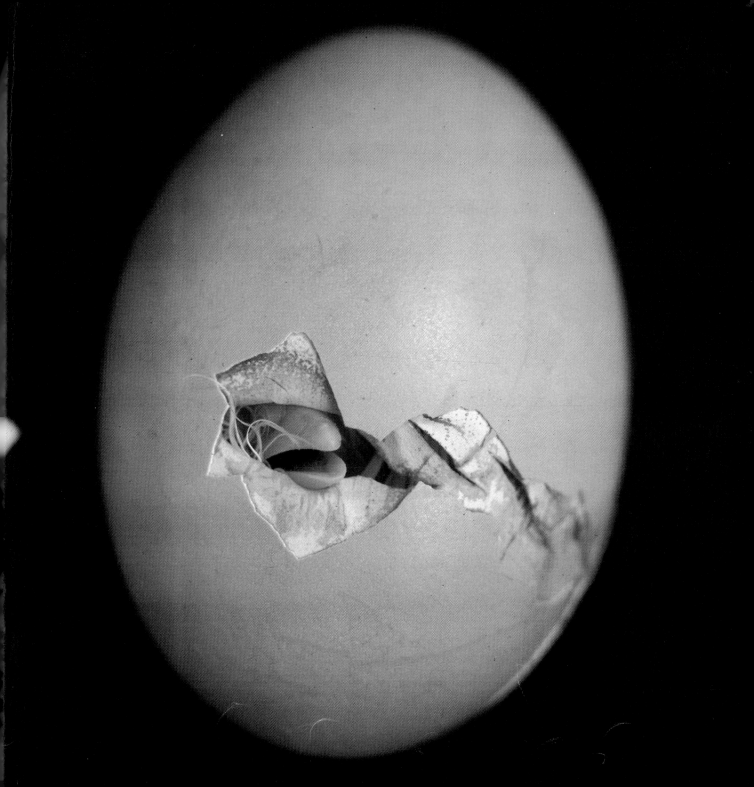

The chick comes out of the eggshell.

At last the shell breaks open.
The chick puts one foot out.

Then the chick comes out of the shell.
It is wet and very tired, so it lies down to rest.

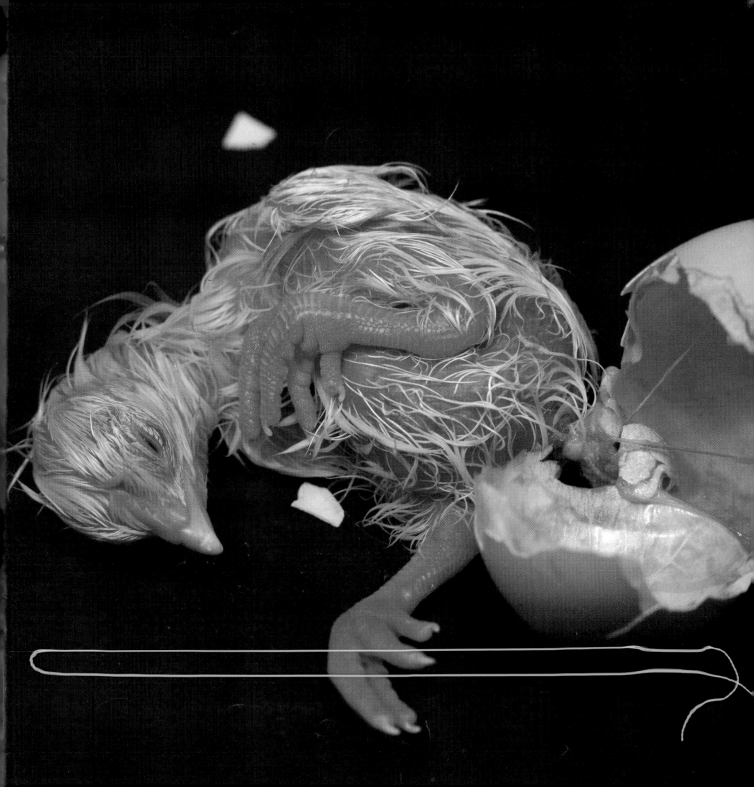

Now the chick is dry. It is soft and fluffy.

Soon the chick can stand up and run around. The chick follows its mother everywhere. It sees the hen peck up food from the ground so it copies her.

The chick will grow up to be a hen or a rooster. If it is a hen, it may mate with a rooster and lay some eggs.

Then what do you think will happen?

Do you remember how the chick grew inside the egg?
See if you can tell the story in your own words.
You can use these pictures to help you.

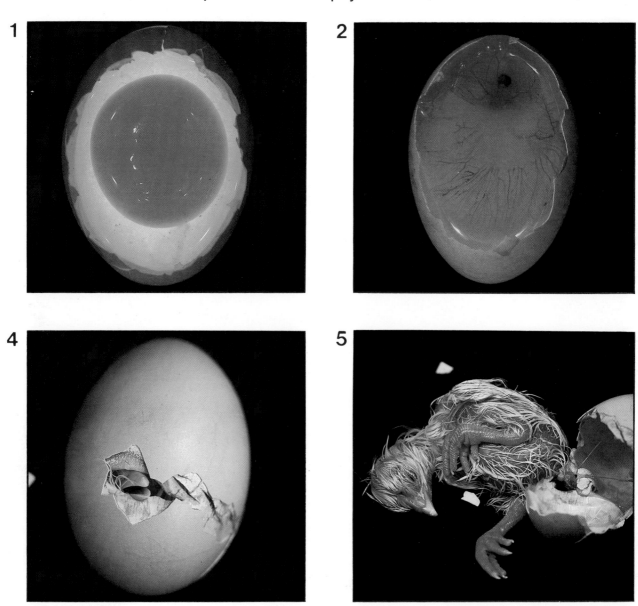

Index

3

6

This index will help you to find some of the important words in the book.

Try cracking an egg. Look at the yolk and the white. Don't forget that chicks do not hatch from eggs that are sold in stores.